Creating and Motivating a Superior, Loyal Staff

National Institute of Business Management, Inc.
1328 Broadway, New York, NY 10001
Printed in U.S.A.

About This Book

For new subscribers like yourself, the purpose of this Book is to present research findings reported to date by the National Institute of Business Management.

It should be noted that while this Book constitutes a compendium of interpersonal techniques—the body of executive skills found to be most closely correlated with major salary advancement—in *current* use by executives, it is your regular twice-monthly issues of WORKING SMART/EXECUTIVE STRATEGIES that will bring you *new* findings as they are made by our continuing research program.

It is a very great pleasure to welcome you, now, as a subscriber to WORKING SMART/EXECUTIVE STRATEGIES, and to the new, fast-evolving world of successful executive practice, which it explains—clearly, simply, quickly—on a continually updated basis that will keep you abreast of changes as they occur.

Copy Desk Chief	Marie Mularczyk
Editorial Assistant	Teri Zucker
Art Director	John Kwong
Graphics Coordinator	Patricia Spieler
Production Manager	Edmund Leisten
Production Assistant	James Hipkiss
Publisher	Brian W. Smith

Creating and Motivating
A Superior, Loyal Staff

Table of Contents

You Can't Beat Upscale, Upbeat Thinking

It's easy—especially when you're down on somebody—to forget the high opinion that virtually everyone has of himself or herself. In their book, *In Search of Excellence* (Harper & Row, NY), Thomas Peters and Robert Waterman, Jr., cite a psychological study in which a random sampling of male adults were asked to rank themselves on "The ability to get along with others."

It turned out, say the authors, that all the participants ranked themselves in the top 10%, and "a full 26% ever so humbly thought they were in the top 1% of the population." In the same study, 70% rated themselves in the top 25% in terms of leadership, and 60% thought they were also in the top 25% in terms of athletic ability.

So much for humility. *Such studies leave little doubt about a deep and pervading vein of self-esteem waiting to be tapped.* "The lesson that the excellent companies have to teach is that...most of their people are made to feel that they are winners," say Peters and Waterman. "Their people, by and large, make their targets and quotas because (these) are set— often by the people themselves—to allow that to happen." An example they use is IBM, "which explicitly manages to ensure that 70%–80% of its salespeople meet quotas, in contrast to a less successful competitor in which only 40% of its sales force meets its quotas in a given year. With this approach, at least 60% of the salespeople think of themselves as losers. Label a man a loser and he'll start acting like one."

Look at your own operation. Is the approach to your people as positive as it could be? Do they think of themselves as winners, or are they constantly being reminded by management that they fall short of organizational goals? If so, here is what you might consider:

- *People tend to act in accordance with their image of themselves.* If they see themselves as well regarded, they will try hard to perpetuate this image. This is where a supportive boss comes in. Praise, appreciation, respect, new responsibilities, delegated authority, bonuses, raises—all these are rewards from you to them that can't help but play a critical role in your employees' sense of self-esteem and their subsequent productivity.

- *People will react bitterly to attacks on their self-esteem.* You can compare the process to the rush of antibodies combating an infection. It's a natural, self-protective reaction that leads, in an organization, to an adversarial relationship between employee and manager, and a counterproductive attitude toward the job. In Peters' and Waterman's book (published in 1982), a General Motors manager is quoted as saying, "Our control systems are designed under the apparent assumption that most of our people are lazy ne'er-do-wells, just waiting to lie, cheat, steal or otherwise screw us. We demoralize 95% of the work force who do act as adults by designing systems to cover our tails against the 5% who really are bad actors."

- *People tend to react positively to positive direction.* There's a crucial difference between correction and criticism. One goes up, the other down. Thus, "You're good at following suggestions," tends to produce a cooperative, ready-to-listen attitude, while "You can't take criticism," tends to bring on opposition. And, "You can do better than this," elicits more of an I'll-try-again response than does, "I'm getting tired of your lousy work."

* *People can surprise you, if given the opportunity.* Even those whom you may consider uncreative can emerge with fresh ideas when you make it clear that you expect this from them; that you'll listen to suggestions, consider new possibilities, and act on and reward whatever advances your operation. But creativity is withheld when the organizational atmosphere says, "Mistakes will not be tolerated; there is no need for new ideas."

Observation: There are always those individuals who, for one reason or another, cannot or will not respond to encouragement, to suggestions, to the possibility of reward. They may lack the interest, energy or capability to do so. But these are exceptions—who shouldn't be allowed to disprove the rule.

News on Today's Participative Systems

I t has become increasingly apparent that the traditional authoritarian style of management in manufacturing operations is losing ground to participative systems that reward workers' input to the management process. And while larger companies have generally led the way by introducing and developing various worker-participation strategies, smaller companies are finding that they can adapt these techniques and programs to suit their own operations.

One such program, Employee Participation Groups (EPGs), introduced by General Motors at several plants, has led to significant improvements in quality and productivity. The backbone of the system is the organization of all the workers of a plant into semiautonomous work groups of 10–15 employees who perform related tasks in one part of the plant. Here are the key elements of the system:

- *Employees work as a team.* By learning each others' jobs, workers provide the company with greater flexibility. For example, if one worker is absent, others from the team take his or her place. This job rotation procedure helps streamline operations and prevents delays on the assembly line.

- *Groups hold prearranged weekly meetings,* but the structure is flexible. If a problem crops up that they want to deal with right away, the workers simply stop work and call a meeting.

- *Management still retains the final word,* but workers are able to organize their work much more than in the past.

- *No one is forced to participate,* even though all plant employees are organized into groups. If a worker wants to do the job and be left alone, that's fine. However, most workers participate in meetings and other group-related activities.

- *Workers keep their own time records.* They also schedule overtime, set certain procedures and standards and decide daily job assignments. Work groups may decide how a job is to be done.

- *Work groups are instrumental in quality control and training.* They decide who is responsible for ensuring the quality of a product and develop ideas for reducing defect rates. When new employees are hired, the work group takes responsibility for their training.

- *Employees receive "pay for knowledge."* That is, they qualify for pay raises by learning more jobs. An employee who has learned all the skills of the team can thus qualify for a pay raise of approximately 50 cents per hour. In general, employees qualify for a given level of compensation by the number of jobs they can perform in a related area.

According to a GM spokesperson, plants using semiautonomous work groups have achieved greater productivity and improved quality over plants not using this system. Furthermore, employees, in general, like participating in group activities. Most workers appreciate the opportunity to contribute their knowledge to improving operations and product quality. What's more, increasing the responsibilities demanded of workers translates directly into greater job satisfaction and a heightened sense of loyalty to the company.

The See-How-It-Goes Approach

T he flight of the human-powered Gossamer Albatross across the English Channel in 1979 was a remarkable and rather unsung feat of American technology, accomplished in direct competition with teams from Japan, England and other countries. The actual construction of the craft was accomplished under unusual managerial circumstances. In his book, *Gossamer Odyssey* (Houghton Mifflin, Boston), Morton Grosser writes about how daily work on the craft was assigned:

"The construction chief, or whoever was acting foreman for the day, would go over to the airplane and write down all the jobs that needed to be done. His list, usually written on several sheets of lined yellow paper taped end-to-end, was then posted on the hangar wall. Whenever someone finished what he was working on, he would stroll over to the list and scan it from top to bottom. 'Hmmm,' was a common audible accompaniment to this survey, followed by 'I guess I can do that.' Most often, (this procedure) resulted in people's doing what they were best at and producing a successful and well-crafted plane in a remarkably short time."

Your own gossamer. Despite the unique objective of the Gossamer project, there is something that managers can learn from its success. This is because there are times when you may find yourself involved in a project for which previous guidelines are scanty—coming up with a market for a novel product, say, or adapting to a new energy source. Whatever it is, you now find yourself forced to start out in a new direction. If this is the case, consider whether some of the approaches that worked in the Gossamer project might be useful. For instance:

- *Can leadership be rated?* What if the posting of assignments, as in the Gossamer project, is handled by one supervisor one day, perhaps by another acting supervisor the next? What rules is necessity and circumstance, not necessarily a prior agenda. Thus, the supervisor who becomes heavily involved in one phase of the project can be relieved of overall responsibility by another member of the team, with no injury to the project. Indeed, there will probably be a net gain because of wider participation in various project phases.

- *Can responsibility be shared?* Each Gossamer project member had to take a periodic—even daily—look at what had been done and what needed to be done. This resulted in members tending to view the project in terms of its progress toward completion, not merely from the viewpoint of their own particular skill or interest.

- *Can project members choose their own assignments?* A rigid management approach would not allow this. In the Gossamer project, however, the result of this self-choosing was a sorting out of talent and personality that produced highly successful results. When an assignment is given to the employee who feels that he or she can do it successfully, the result can be a highly motivated individual who learns fast and accomplishes much.

Observation: Special circumstances for a manager can call for a special approach. True, you can't discard every management practice that's worked for you in the past. But you can experiment with one or two new ideas—and see how it goes.

When Your Staff Succeeds, So Do You

Herman W. Lay, entrepreneur and super salesman, had a business career that spanned more than four decades. Two of his chief accomplishments: developing the first national brand of potato chips and, as head of the Frito-Lay Company, helping to establish Pepsico, the giant conglomerate.

What was the key to his success? One of his closest associates saw it this way: "It was his interest in people and in seeing people succeed—he gave people responsibility and then left them alone to do the job."

Giving people responsibility—leaving them alone to do the job—is something that many managers don't do. For one reason or another, they handle all the big jobs, all the important work, themselves. Or, when they do hand over a big assignment, they hover over its recipient, constantly checking and rechecking, giving directions, making changes, generally running the whole show. True, the job gets done, but in the end, neither the manager nor the employee gains very much.

Self-examination. Perhaps there have been times when you have noticed a similar tendency in yourself. Rather than handing over an important project and letting a qualified assistant go it alone, you have either added it to your own busy schedule or stayed very much in charge as the individual struggled to get it done.

This is a tendency that is generally characteristic of managers who don't realize how important it is to their own development and promotability to have a staff that is capable of growth, of doing a larger job. So the next time you find yourself leaning back from giving an assistant an opportunity, ask yourself some stock-taking questions:

- *What am I afraid of?* Managers who are reluctant to delegate can usually come up with what they consider to be logical explanations for their stand. . . "He won't be able to get it done on time". . . "She's bound to make some mistake". . . "I can do it better and faster." But explanations of this kind are based on the fear of letting go, of losing control. As such, they are neither realistic nor practical—and they are also not helpful.

Determine just what it is that you're afraid of—and then ask yourself:

- *What have I got to lose?* The answer to this depends, of course, on the nature and importance of the job. In some cases, you might stand to lose a great deal if the job isn't handled successfully. But consider this: You can give an employee a basic idea of what needs to be done, you can build in deadlines, and you can stand by to provide assistance if it's necessary. These are all safeguards that can help to ensure that the job gets done right—and on time.

After you've thought through this aspect of delegating work, ask yourself:

- *What have I got to gain?* Chances are, a great deal. For one thing, you have lifted a heavy burden off your own

-11-

shoulders—and this gives you more time for other jobs. True, you may have some worrisome moments, but that's a small price to pay for not having to take everything on yourself.

Far more important, though, is the fact that you will be helping an employee earn the chance to develop and grow. In giving someone responsibility and leaving him or her alone to do the job, you will be making an important contribution to that person's eventual success—not to mention your own. Why? Because managers who make it clear that only they can do a particular job are liable to be stuck with that responsibility permanently.

Managers Draw Power from the "Power of Example"

T he scenario: The economic climate has forced upper
management to tighten the organizational belt. Middle
managers are transferred or terminated and various operations combined. Remaining staff is forced to share offices
and secretaries, and raises are postponed. All employees feel
the uncertainty and strain as they work harder and longer,
and worry whether their own jobs will be the next to go.

If your company is experiencing lean times, this scenario
may sound familiar, and you may feel these pressures too.
When your boss is under the gun to do more with less, and
expects the same of you, you in turn must require *more* of
your employees. At the same time, you might feel yourself
to be the target of others' accumulated frustrations. What
can you do to preserve your equanimity without resorting
to kicking the proverbial dog—your staff?

The fact is, you can take control. You can gauge your actions and attitudes so that they boost your own morale as
well as that of others. The way you handle yourself can mean
the difference between an atmosphere of fear and blame and
one of confidence and cooperation. How can you accomplish
this? For starters, consider these simple suggestions:

• *Set an example.* Attitudes from above can be crucial. When the emotional climate at the top is negative, your behavior can set the tone for subordinates. Let's suppose that your boss handles stress poorly and makes what you consider unreasonable requests, such as giving up a holiday or planned vacation, or doing the work of a laid-off assistant. A response that shows tolerance for your boss's frustrations will help create an atmosphere of understanding and support that everyone needs. Conversely, reacting with anger is likely to elicit an angry response and erode your relationship with your boss and, eventually, your employees. But if you can control your own resentment, you will be setting an example for your employees to do the same when circumstances require *you* to put stronger demands on *them*.

- *Speak clearly, listen closely.* When an organization is under stress, rumors abound and tempers run short. In such an atmosphere, clear communication with people above and below you is especially important. With both types of communication, it's essential to clear up rumors before they grow and become ungovernable.

- *Avoid apologies.* You will undoubtedly have to ask more of your staff than you would normally find equitable. In this event, remember that an apologetic stance can be just as unproductive as one that shows your resentment. Both attitudes are demotivators, and they diminish the respect you need in order to manage effectively.

When you have tough orders to carry out, remind your staff that everyone is under similar pressure; that all, including you and your boss, must do unpleasant things and that it's important to act in unison to help get the company back on track to save jobs. The best way to impart this kind of news is in face-to-face meetings, rather than through impersonal memos or casual remarks. When you are assertive in this way, the net effect is often to encourage rather than discourage people.

* *Enhance your visibility.* Difficult times present an opportunity to show management that you are a team player, willing to pull your weight and make sacrifices for the organization. You can demonstrate your adaptability and versatility when you take on another function without missing a beat, cover a transferred manager's department while boosting production in your own or devise ways to keep morale high among your staff. The chances are now much greater that your efforts will be noticed—and appreciated.

Observation: It could also be helpful to adjust your outlook and regard the situation as temporary. You might set a date, two or three months away, on which you will reassess matters if the crunch has not eased, to see if another course is warranted. For the present, though, if an extraordinary effort is called for, your best bet is to respond with your utmost.

Use Incentives to Boost Productivity

Many managers, at a loss as to how to make their employees more productive, long for the sort of power that would force them to produce—or else. Yet, if the ability to impose raw will on subordinates is a measure of productivity, then the Soviet Union should long since have been leading the world in the production and exportation of goods of all sorts. The fact is, though, that few Soviet products have much of an impact on world markets.

What makes it difficult for Soviet managers to really succeed, say various experts, is the lack of incentives. In the Soviet Union, it doesn't seem to matter very much whether you work hard or not; the result, say these observers, is pretty much the same—poor food, poor housing, poor prospects. Those who do work hard, therefore, are thought to be foolish by their co-workers. The upshot is today's Russia, whose economy is considered closer to a Third World country than to a western nation.

The advantage. By Soviet standards, managers here enjoy a wide and still effective range of incentives to offer an employee. Consider the following:

• *Purchasing power.* The goods and services and real property that can be obtained by working in this country rank close to the top on a world scale. More money is still a powerful incentive that you can use—not only in the form of raises but also, on a deeper level, as it is used in profit-sharing and stock-purchase plans.

* *The value of a job.* Where there are more jobs than there are workers, as in the Soviet Union, managers can't use job security as an incentive. But where it is widely recognized that good jobs are not so easy to find or keep, those who have jobs that they value become sensitive to the connection between individual productivity and organizational survival. If you can point out this connection to employees without intimidating them, you're utilizing a powerful incentive.

* *Recognition of effort, access to higher levels.* The employee who does superior work will continue to work on this level when it's recognized and appreciated. You can support this process with praise, trust and promotion. The opportunity to provide encouragement and upward mobility continues to rank high in the hierarchy of incentives.

* *The excitement and responsibility of management.* Employee self-interest and organizational goals tend to merge when employees can participate in management's decision-making and decision-implementing processes. This is the force behind quality circles. And despite the complications and barriers presented by the traditional management system, such participation is a developing road to managers who know how powerful this incentive can be.

Observation: There is an obviously self-defeating way to look at potential incentives. That is, to regard them as a means to intimidate employees, rather than to encourage them. But the temptation to do this can be overcome by self-examination—how do *you*, as an employee, respond to threats of a cut in pay, the loss of your job, the loss of an opportunity to advance? Probably not by working harder and better, but by covering your tracks, playing it safe and shifting the blame to others; by doing less and making it look like more. This is why incentives are best used only as encouragement. Also, most people can readily perceive a downward slide without being told about it.

Has Your Authority Sprung a Leak?

Y ou have been aware of the situation for some time now: bits and pieces of overheard conversations, some rather telling comments from your boss and cryptic glances from some employees. Putting them all together, they seem to add up to one thing: One or more of the people who report to you are going behind your back; taking ideas, complaints, whatever, directly to your boss.

But though you are aware of *what* is happening, you don't know *why* it is happening. "And that's something I'm going to have to find out," you tell yourself. "I'm getting it from both sides—and I have to find a way to put an end to it." Now, you wonder, just what is the best approach to take in a situation of this kind?

No hasty moves. So far, you have realized an important truth for managers—the need to deal with an upsetting and potentially dangerous situation. Failure to do so could indicate the undermining of your position in the organization, the eventual erosion of your authority. But, whatever your present situation, it would not be wise to do anything hastily. You might say or do something ineffectual or self-damaging that you would regret later. Rather, you—or any manager in a similar position—would do well to take time first to answer, as objectively as possible, these two very important questions:

- *What kind of relationship do you presently have with your boss?* Many people make the mistake of thinking that any working relationship—be it with a boss, a colleague or a subordinate—continues on an even keel. If it was good yesterday, it must also be good today. But most such relationships veer in different directions from time to time—from good to bad to better, depending upon people and circumstances.

It could be, therefore, that the relationship between you and your boss isn't what you thought it was. It could be that you have done something to cause him or her anger. Or, it could be that there is a kind of power play involved—your boss may actually be encouraging people to come directly to her (or him) in an attempt to gain more power, and possibly do you in. Thinking over the situation may reveal some problems that you hadn't realized existed.

- *What kind of relationship do you presently have with the people who report to you?* There has to be some reason why people circumvent their immediate bosses. Sometimes, of course, it may be just a ploy to ingratiate themselves with top management. More often, though, it's due to the subordinates' belief that their bosses don't want to listen to their ideas, don't want to hear their complaints and don't want to be concerned with their problems, because they haven't the power to do anything about them.

Are you open with the people who report to you—and do they feel that they can be honest with you? Are you willing to do something about their complaints and provide them with assistance for their problems? Do you encourage people to come to you with ideas and suggestions? In analyzing the situation—again, as objectively as possible—you may find that you have been raising barriers between yourself and the people who report to you. Not intentionally, perhaps, but nonetheless they are still there.

Stepping forward. In line with your evaluation of the situation, you may then want to take the following steps:

- *Get on a better footing with your boss.* This will call for some decisive action on your part—you can't expect your boss to make the first move. Make it a point to consult him or her on special problems. Discuss some of your ideas. Ask for backing on a project you would like to undertake. Do all this in person—and do it in an open, friendly manner.

Should you discuss with your boss the fact that certain employees have been going behind your back? Probably not at first. But as your working relationship improves, you might bring it up and conclude with: "I'd appreciate it if, when something like that occurs again, you would simply refer that person back to me."

- *Encourage people to come to you.* This may take some doing at first, particularly if you have fallen into the habit of shutting people off—or out. You might start by calling them into your office to talk over a problem—and you might stop by their offices to discuss ideas. Your aim should be to make them feel that your door is open and your mind is receptive to their thinking. Equally important, you are ready to act on that thinking, when appropriate—be it in dealing with a complaint, pushing for a solution to a problem or putting good ideas to immediate use.

When people come to realize that you are indeed in charge, and ready and willing to hear them out, it's very likely that they will see no further reason for going around you to get to your boss. They'll see *you* as the boss.

Solid Managers Give Solid Answers

You know from experience that being able to count on a straight answer from your boss makes your own work as a manager easier. And yet, for a variety of reasons, you may not feel that you are responding to those who report to you with the same kind of decisiveness you value from your own boss.

You may feel this way because a straight answer to a question is, ideally, a clear-cut yes or no. But when that is not possible, a straight answer can also be an explanation of what needs to be done before such an answer becomes possible. Here's how it would work, depending on circumstances:

- *When you need time to weigh the consequences.* This is a valid concern; when assistants want something out of the ordinary, they don't always consider what kind of precedent may be set or how the request might be disruptive. Such considerations are vital before coming to a decision, and it is legitimate to require time to work them out. But that doesn't mean that you have to reply in an indecisive fashion.

  Straight answer: Tell the person what your caveats are. He or she just may have anticipated them and have information that will help you reach a decision. If you have to do this research on your own, tell the person what you have to do beforehand and when you will have a decision, and then keep your promise.

- *When you need to discuss it with your boss or another manager to be on safe ground.* Too hasty a decision can get you into trouble. There are bases that have to be covered and contingencies to be discussed.

Straight answer: Tell the person whom you have to consult and promise to let him or her know when you have done so—setting a time or date if possible.

- *When saying yes right away might make you appear to be an easy mark and similar requests could escalate.* You know right away that you will agree to the request. In this case, there's no need to drag out the time between the request and the reply.

Straight answer: Say yes while setting limits. For example, if an employee needs extra time off for a family emergency, you might say: "Yes, I will see that you're covered for tomorrow, but we absolutely need you here for the meeting on Thursday."

- *When an outright no seems harsh and you'd rather let the person down gradually.* You're keeping the person on tenterhooks, still hoping you'll say yes when you know you will say no. This is really less kind—straight doesn't have to be harsh.

Straight answer: Say no and then explain the valid reasons why not. "I simply cannot grant your request for another employee in your unit this year; the budget doesn't have any slack."

- *When the request is vague.* "Do you think I might get some assistance soon?'' But a vague request needn't call for a vague answer.

Straight answer: Ask questions back. ''What assistance do you need?'' Let the person know where the gaps are, what additional information is necessary in order for you to answer the question in a sensible way.

Observation: In all cases, you are giving your staff something substantial. It's the feeling that the boss is up front, in control and reasonable. In the end, this is what employees really want.

You Can't Toy with Your Own Authority

Near the end of a successful spring training, Doug Sisk, a relief pitcher for the New York Mets, heard talk that he might make the staff. But then the equipment manager told the rookie that George Bamberger, who was then the Mets manager, wanted to see him. Sisk wondered what he had done. He remembers Bamberger saying, "Sorry Doug, I can't keep you. You've got to report to Tidewater. Do you have anything that you want to say?"

"No, George," said Sisk.

"That's good," said Bamberger, "because that's not how it is. You're staying."

Thereupon Sisk's teammates, who had huddled outside the office listening to this prank, broke up with laughter, and Sisk went on to make the team.

There is, of course, nothing wrong with fun and laughter. But there just may be something a bit wrongheaded about a manager who uses the upper hand to play games with an employee's anxiety about job security. People may not want to exert themselves or take coaching from someone who demonstrates this degree of insensitivity.

If you are a manager who wants to be sure that your employees remain fully receptive to your direction, here's what you might keep in mind:

- *Your words and actions are magnified by your authority.*

Just about everything your employees observe about you is a bit larger than life and often seems more important to them than you intended. Thus, what may only mean a bit of teasing to you may indicate to one of your employees an entire attitude, a cast of mind; a bias that, from your viewpoint, is dangerously distorted.

- *Your humor can have aftereffects.* There is recourse when a peer makes fun of you, puts you down or says something discomfitingly off color. You can reply in kind, or say, simply, that you've had enough. It's harder to do this with your boss—especially when, as with Doug Sisk, you feel that the person who is managing you has all the power and you have none. So, you say nothing and appear to be a good sport—but there may be plenty that you communicate to others later that has a negative effect on their attitude and subsequent performance.

- *There is no substitute for seriousness of purpose.* Again, there is nothing wrong with laughter—it loosens tensions, strengthens common bonds and can even serve as a rallying point. But it does not take the place of the kind of managerial intensity that arouses equal intensity in one's staff, that ignites a spark. Too often, it can have the opposite effect—making such extra effort and dedication seem a bit silly.

Observation: No matter what, it's hard to be anyone but yourself when you manage. If you're given to humor, to kidding around, to teasing, then so be it. It's best to manage in the most natural style possible. But it pays to remember that what worked for you among peers may not be appropriate for your employees.

What if There's Dissension Down Below?

People who work together are not necessarily personal friends. Some people, indeed, can work quite competently and productively with those they actually dislike. So the way staff members feel about each other need not be a matter of great concern to a manager—unless some animosities get out of hand. What's out of hand? Consider the following situations:

...Key staffers are not speaking to each other.

...Hostile camps exist.

...Who does what has become a matter of who is friendly with whom.

...Staffers resist assignments outside of their traditional responsibilities.

...Key information is held closely by a small subgroup.

If such counterproductive situations exist in your group, you probably need to intervene. Very often, a thoughtful manager can reduce the effects of feuding and political position taking, but it isn't easy. Here are some suggestions to get you started:

- *Make your message clear.* You want people to cooperate. This message from the boss is most heeded if the hostilities in your group are not widespread, but limited to only two or three people. Consider holding a small and pleasant meeting together to discuss the ongoing problem.

- *Be equitable in your attention,* so that those who are feuding don't feel that you're on one side or the other. This, along with your previous directive to cooperate, will strengthen your point.

- *Tell them what you want.* Sometimes a direct order is most effective. Sit down with feuding employees, discuss how animosity is hampering the work of the group and upsetting others. Offer whatever help they feel is needed to iron out the issues that separate them.

- *Identify a common cause.* People who are at odds with each other can be brought together by a common purpose. This could be some healthy competition with another organization or a deadline that is in everyone's interest to achieve.

- *Restructure jobs,* so that people must cooperate in order to accomplish their objectives. On the other hand, if you decide that working together is impossible, you could find ways of making their work autonomous, as little dependent upon each other as possible to complete the assignment.

Observation: There are also those situations in which nothing that you, the manager, can do will help. In such cases, it's undoubtedly best that those who are involved work it out for themselves—provided the job is getting done.

Controls Are Important— But So Is Judgment

Y ou may think that what you need most right now is greater control over your operation. You may be right—as long as you don't make the same mistake a Chicago manager finally realized he had made. Some months after he initiated an elaborate system to determine whether his lower-level managers were doing what he wanted, it suddenly occurred to him that while they were working harder than ever to get out the reports he requested, they were accomplishing less overall. He also realized that his own productivity had declined, and that he had carefully devised a system to produce the opposite of what he intended.

To many managers, ''control'' means requiring approval before allowing important activities to take place; or knowing, with varying degrees of detail, what employees are producing, compared with what they are supposed to be producing. Unfortunately, many operations languish as a result of taking the medicine that was supposed to cure what ailed them. Here's what can go wrong:

• *You may spend more on the effort to control than you can possibly get in return.* A new manager, faced with a request from one unit's supervisor for a costly microcomputer, acknowledged that the equipment seemed very promising as a way to solve some serious problems the unit had, but asked for a detailed justification of the request. Between the work involved in preparing the report, answering questions about it, going out to get more information that had been requested and holding many meetings to thrash out uncertainties, not only did the cost of staff time exceed the cost of the equipment, but the problems also continued unabated for many months.

- *You may wind up getting more information than you can handle.* Then you face the uneasy choice of either spending more of your time reading reports or laying aside unread reports that subordinates, who expect a reaction from you, have gone to great trouble to prepare.

- *You may assume that you have accomplished your job as a manager when you institute controls,* even though you need more than controls if you want to see results. You may have overlooked sensible corrective action. "My boss flies into a rage when I report more than three trucks out of service," comments one motor fleet manager. "But the problem is the age of the trucks and the number of mechanics needed to work on them. Since no one wants to do anything about this, the situation will be no better when the next report is due."

- *You may not get accurate information if your subordinates are uneasy about what you'll do with it.* Even reasonably honest people won't bring any rope if they think you may hang them. A new manager responsible for investigating insurance claims used an ingenious way of counting to show that her office had few problems with backlogged claims. She simply counted as "backlogs" only those cases that she had not yet assigned to investigators. Thus, several hundred cases that had been assigned but never started, or were still not closed nine months later, never showed in the count and kept her records looking good.

- *You may be getting information that you used to need, but that you don't need now.* Many managers feel reassured that their authority is still intact when they continue to receive reams of irrelevant information. They overlook the effort that is wasted in getting it together and sending it—effort better used elsewhere.

So, to sum it up, though you must have control over the operation for which you're responsible, too much control can be unhealthy—stultifying to the initiative of your employees, breeding their resistance, taking more of their time (and yours) than you can justify and costing more than it can save. What do you have to do to exercise controls effectively? Some suggestions:

- *Keep it simple.* Don't ask for more information than you can digest, or more than your subordinates can readily give you.

- *Only control what needs controlling.* The dictum—"If it ain't broke, don't fix it"—may be extreme, especially for managers who believe in preventive maintenance, but it contains much wisdom. Because you can't control everything around you, choose those things that make a significant difference to the health of your company, those areas where there's a danger that without controls something might seriously go wrong.

- *Think carefully whether your means of control are help-*

ing or hurting. If your approval is needed for every initiative, and you are too busy to give each one your attention, you can be a bottleneck.

- *Let people in on the purpose.* They can cooperate with you more fully if they know what use you're making of requested information. At the same time, they can let you know how the controls are affecting their work.

- *Let assistants control what they can, instead of having to come to you.* Your assistants are undoubtedly closer to the details of their operation than you are, and are thus in a position to spot problems immediately and do what has to be done. You are the gainer when they feel that it's *their* job—not just yours—to note when quality is slipping, deadlines are not being met or costs are being exceeded.

- *Consider whether you are giving signals that do not jibe with the controls you set.* One manager regularly kept staffers cooling their heels in his outer office for a half hour or more until he began meetings. At the same time, he also insisted that they strictly enforce the policy that their own employees return from lunch on time, because ''time is money.'' It's hard to convince people that you mean what you say if you are not personally consistent with your own philosophy.

Observation: Management thinking on the subject of controls has undergone several swings in direction over time—from the view that controls meant constant observation and elaborate report systems, to the notion that subordinates needed direction and help much more than they needed controls, to today's more realistic idea that controls should be used, but only when they are needed; and only with those people for whom they're needed. In other words, as little as possible.

Those Down-Putting Comments Can Do You Harm

Y ou've heard how a colleague has made a fool of himself or herself, and you can't wait to share the episode;
. . . The manager of another department has tried your patience to its limit, and you absolutely must let off some steam;
. . . Your boss has been grossly unfair once again, and you want to spread the word about the latest victimization;
. . . Another manager asks you for your opinion of a colleague who habitually rubs you the wrong way.

Dangers ahead. Temptations to make negative comments about those with whom you work are varied and frequent. Yet, the wisest course is to resist. You may want to say it, you may trust the discretion of your listener and your opinion may be founded in fact. Nevertheless, it is still in your own best interest to bite your tongue, purse your lips and think matters over before you utter a word.

There is a variety of reasons why the negatives you transmit about others can do you direct harm. Consider some of the possibilities:

- *You could have it wrong*—particularly if what you're passing on is something you heard from someone else.

- *Circumstances could change.* The person in another department today could become your colleague—or even your boss—tomorrow.

- *You could be incurring distrust.* That you are speaking negatively about someone could by itself be the quality that impresses your listener most—not the actual content of what you are saying. As a result, listeners could well be forming negative impressions of you—for example, that you are indiscreet, or that you might speak in the same way about them.

- *Your words could be used against you.* Even if you are talking in confidence with someone you trust, you never know when and to whom your words will be repeated— or misquoted.

- *Your negativism can be perceived as being your attitude.* Your remarks may be funny, apt and accurate but, as the saying goes, nobody likes a wise guy. People are put off by those who continually seem to treat serious matters as a joke, or who miss no opportunity to pass on negative information about a colleague or boss.

Observation: Saying only nice things is nice, but not a good idea. There *are* times when it is honestly satisfying and useful to convey negative information. But a particular tone of voice, a shrug or a conspicuous silence can tell your listener much of what you're thinking without getting yourself into unnecessary trouble. If you must, reluctantly, speak ill of another person, be sure you have given the possible reaction some thought. It could prevent a lot of trouble later.

What's a Busy Manager to Do About Approachability?

Few managers nowadays have more time than they know what to do with. Quite the contrary, in fact, which is undoubtedly why a manager from Delaware writes: "What does a busy manager do to look approachable to his staff in the face of a hectic schedule and lots going on? As second in command of a small state agency, I have more to do than I can get done. Even so, I have been told more than once by someone I trust that I have a reputation for being stand-offish and intimidating. This is hard for me to take, because I think of myself as a person who is inclined to help others. Is there something I could be doing to change what seems to be my present image into one that more closely represents the person who is really me?"

Possibilities. Though it sometimes seems that way, you don't have to be a manager to be unapproachable. In any organization, there are employees who have only the most minimal contact with others, and who do not complain about this state of affairs. They have, so it would seem, arrived at what is a state of equilibrium for them. Presumably, neither they nor their employers feel they have to be "approachable" to do a satisfactory job.

Should it be any different for a manager? Well, if management is truly the art of getting things done through other people, then a manager must, to some degree, be approachable. But before you make any sudden changes, or torment yourself with thoughts that you are not as approachable as you ought to be—or as other people tell you that you ought to be—here are some ideas to consider:

- Some people won't feel comfortable with a boss who suddenly wants to be approached, particularly when they have learned to live with a boss who is not all that approachable.

- While some managers are more approachable than others, our editors know no studies proving that these more approachable managers have more productive employees than do less approachable managers.

- There are many managerial styles, just as there are many personal styles. Whatever style has worked for you until now is likely to work for you in the future as well.

- If you really want to be more approachable, you can begin by staying in your office less and in other people's offices more.

You can continue by seeking out other people whenever the opportunity arises, especially those with whom you're uncomfortable. Emphasize meetings—either face to face or on the phone—rather than memos. Take advantage of chance encounters, even though they may *not* be what you think is appropriate in a boss-employee relationship.

Observation: Once you start on a course of more approachability than you formerly enjoyed, you won't be able to check the results unless you stick with it. A day or a week of enhanced approachability isn't long enough. A minimum of six months is a more reasonable time span for acclimating yourself and your employees to this new role, and evaluating what comes out of it.

Heavy-Handed Supervision Often Misses the Mark

Experienced managers know that when disciplinary measures are laid on with a heavy hand, they may become counterproductive. The supervisor who makes the most noise about lateness, for example, is not necessarily the one whose group has the best on-time performance record. When a note from a doctor is insisted on for every absence, absenteeism doesn't necessarily decline. Safety measures are not always best practiced by employees whose supervisors threaten penalties for noncompliance. Telephone courtesy is not always best under the direction of a supervisor who habitually checks up by listening in on calls.

The reason. One good explanation for such seemingly paradoxical behavior is that extreme disciplinary measures can have the unintended effect of making employees feel less accountable for others in their group who may be breaking rules. Too much pressure from a supervisor may cause them to be disinclined to exert peer pressure of their own. In one study of theft by employees, for example, it was found that in many operations where security measures were not strict or enforced, employees themselves discouraged theft by co-workers.

In light of this, it might be a good idea to look into the

observance of rules in your own organization. Perhaps your supervisors could benefit from the following suggestions:

- *Make your policy clear.* Unless supervisors are certain that the organization cares about clarity, they themselves have a less-than-compelling reason to care about whether disciplinary matters are understood. Most of the companies that had enjoyed the lowest theft rates in the study mentioned above also had clearly defined company policies. This is why standards of punctuality, attendance and other work prerequisites should be spelled out, rather than assumed to be understood.

- *Rules should be explained by supervisors.* For reminders about rules to be most effective, they should come to the employees from their direct supervisors and include the reasons behind them—the high costs of inventory losses, for example, or of overtime necessitated by undue absenteeism, or the burden that latecomers put on fellow employees.

- *Encourage supervisors to strive for employee cooperation.* The supervisor who trusts—and is trusted by—employees in the course of daily work is the one most likely to inspire peer pressure among employees to observe good organizational behavior. The supervisor who does everything by edict will likely have trouble in this respect.

- *Encourage supervisors to enforce rules evenly.* If a rule is there, it must be enforced without exception if people are to respect any company rules. As for penalties, the theft study also found that even relatively mild punishments were strong deterrents—but only when administered without exception.

Observation: If there are some disciplinary rules that your supervisors do not enforce regularly, this may reflect poorly on the rule rather than on them. Discuss with your supervisors which rules are realistic to enforce and which would be better altered.

Your Assistants Should Be Acting as Your Agents

G enerally speaking, those managers who insist that their orders be carried out in an exact and literal fashion, whose assistants are not encouraged to think for themselves, are the managers who are likely to complain that "I have to do it all," or "I have to be here all the time."

Such managers are also often the target of what one management expert calls "malicious obedience." Assistants who are resentful at being treated as if they were brainless will implement orders that they know will do damage or cause trouble.

What's the remedy? Obviously, it's a staff that can act sensibly whether you're there or not, a staff willing and able to act on your behalf—even when you're in error.

Here are some ways in which this can be developed:

* *State your expectations.* Don't assume that your assistants—particularly those who are new—are going to know what attitude you want them to have. Thus, you might say, "Eileen, when I'm in a hurry, or have something else on my mind, when what I ask you to do needs to be questioned, I'd appreciate it if you would ask me or whoever else is available about it, because I may just be making a horrendous mistake at that point and need

to change things around. Okay?''

- *Listen to objections.* If you want to be corrected by an assistant when the need arises (and it will), then make your reaction positive, even though one of your instructions or proposals is being questioned. This may take some self-control, but the benefits are worth it. It is possible, no matter how much irritation you may feel at having a decision questioned, to thank the assistant who says, ''It seems to me that shipping that large quantity seems risky in this kind of credit situation. Can't we hold off for a day or two and check a little further?''

Or you might thank the secretary who deliberately delays typing your peppery reply to a complaining customer, so that you can have time to see the wisdom of writing something more diplomatic.

- *Share your thinking.* Your assistants should know what standards your judgments are based upon if they're going to be able to spot when you're going astray. They should also know whether they've done the right thing or the wrong thing when they act on your behalf. So make it clear to them when you agree or disagree with their judgment.

Observation: While it's great to get good assistance, this doesn't mean you should try to solicit your assistant's approval before a decision can be made. After all, running the operation is *your* responsibility—which is why you are the manager. But if you share your thinking with your assistants, they are likely to do the same with you. The result can only lead to better decisions and fewer mistakes—particularly of the kind that are malicious.

Don't Assume That Intervention Is Always Necessary

O ne remarkable aspect of professional hockey to an unschooled observer is the way referees allow the players to fight. Usually, they step in and separate the combatants only after they've hit each other a few times. Hockey aficionados explain this behavior by saying that if referees stepped between two would-be combatants immediately, not only would they be dampening the excitement, but they would also be likely to receive the blows meant for the players. By letting the antagonists go at each other, they're looking out for themselves.

Forbearance of this sort makes a good deal of sense, and not only for hockey referees. Managers, too, sometimes find themselves in situations where they could intervene and break up a possible battle. But, as in hockey, too fast an intervention could be counterproductive. So, if you are on the edge of a combat zone in your organization, and have the authority or inclination to intervene, here's what you might consider before actually stepping in:

- *Could I benefit by holding back?* Two of your staff members have a long history of disagreeing with each other. At the same time, they're both employees whom you value. Occasionally, in the course of a meeting, their ill will raises the room temperature. You could, of course, step in immediately with, "That's enough of that, you two." Chances are they will subside, but it may be with the feeling that they haven't been given the chance to fully express themselves openly, and that you are the sort of boss who can't take anything but amity and agreement. Additionally, everyone might be missing out on the kind of excitement that could make the rest of the meeting more productive.

- *Can you learn more than you otherwise might have?* Mutual combat has a way of bringing out, if not the real truth, then certainly what the combatants feel is the truth. You may, for instance, learn of a longstanding grievance that you hadn't known about, or an operational error that had been kept under cover. Such information has a way of not being shared with the boss, even when it could be of great help to you to know about such matters.

- *Can those who are involved straighten it out without you?* Sometimes, it takes a fight to bring about a more amicable relationship. People who have drifted into a mutual dislike, who have become uncommunicative with each other as a result, can find themselves feeling more warmth toward each other after an honest battle.

- *Will you be in the middle?* Everybody knows what can happen when you step into the middle of a fight between a husband and wife. It can rapidly turn into a situation where both turn on the supposed peacemaker. Let's imagine that you've just joined a task force, or a similar organizational group, whose members tend to indulge in rancorous yet productive discussion. If this is their style, and it works, you'll do well to proceed with caution.

Observation: On the whole, fights are to be avoided. Too often, they leave a residue of bad feelings and mutual distaste that is harmful to everyone. But combat is nonetheless a component of human character, and it can have its positive side. Those managers who realize this usually have more understanding and tolerance of the way people in organizations function—even when they are combative.

You Need to Be Told About the Bad Stuff

" " Some of my supervisors seem to feel that I should be shielded from reality," writes a New Jersey manager. "They think they're doing me a favor when they don't tell me about a problem that might go away before I find out about it. As a result, I've had to deal with a few matters regarding suppliers and certain employees that I should have known about long before I was informed. If I had, what became big problems could have remained little ones.

"I've told my staff not to hold back on me like this, but I'm not really sure I'm getting through to them. In my opinion, they are still taking the attitude that what I don't know won't hurt me. What can you tell me about changing this state of affairs?"

Can you handle it? Simply telling your key employees that you want to hear the bad news along with the good is seldom enough. They have to be reassured that they won't be the victim of what a political commentator has called the George Ball Syndrome (Ball, a former Undersecretary of State, was allegedly fired by Lyndon Johnson when Ball told the then President that the U.S. could not win the war in Vietnam). Unless your behavior indicates that you can handle negative information with fairness and equanimity, they are not likely to tell you about it. As the boss, your goodwill is too important to be risked—unless you actually prove that no risk is involved. With this in mind, here's how you might go about encouraging the delivery of news that is not good:

- *Make it easy for employees to see you at any time.* The manager who plays the part of the remote individual who can only be approached on the proper occasion is not going to hear any day-to-day details of an operation—unless the news is decidedly positive. Anything that is negative will tend to be buried until it can be quietly fixed. It's not so much that your assistants don't think you can handle such information as it is their conviction that you want to be shielded from its effect so that you can concentrate on other, supposedly more important matters. If you don't want this "filter" to operate, then make sure you're available and staying in circulation.

- *Ask the right questions.* You probably won't find out what's wrong by asking, "How are things going?" All you're likely to get is an optimistic and uninformative answer. Ask, instead, a question that deals with specifics: "How is your new assistant working out?" or, "Are the new modifications as helpful as you thought they'd be?" Questions like these convey the idea that you're familiar enough with the operation to be told its more intimate details without being bowled over. In this position, chances are better that you'll get the full picture.

- *Avoid the "solution-only" trap.* You may have made it clear that you expect your assistants to present problems to you only when they are accompanied by a clear-cut course of action that you need only approve—or disapprove. Perhaps you did this to avoid the danger of assistants delegating their work upward to you. But there are times when your experience and grasp of wider possibilities can have a vitally positive effect on this problem-solving process. So, be careful about any words or attitude of yours that might indicate too quickly that you feel this is their problem, not yours. It's better to wait until the ensuing discussion is over before deciding.

- *Reward the bearer.* It's not easy to express enthusiasm when you're being given a piece of bad news, but it is possible. The next time it happens, instead of wincing and acting as if the sky has just fallen in, or saying, "Why didn't you tell me this sooner?" you might try, "I'm glad you came to me with this," or "This could have been much worse if you'd waited before you told me." If you can make the bearer feel that you are appreciative because he or she has done the right thing, then you can expect more of the same in the future.

Observation: Basically, managers' chances of getting negative information from employees depend on the kind of relationship they have developed and maintained. A hostile or remote relationship promotes the withholding of information—even though it may ultimately be to the employee's disadvantage. But a friendly and sustained relationship encourages employees to come to the boss with whatever they think is important—good or bad.

Trying to Get Rid of Some White Elephants?

T ina is an elephant who lived for many years in the confined quarters of New York City's Central Park Zoo. When the zoo closed for remodeling, all the larger animals were easily placed in other zoos—except Tina, who exhibited such aggressive behavior against her keepers that no zoo wanted her. Finally, Marine World/Africa USA in Redwood City, California, did take her. She thrived there. She learned to lie down on command, raise her feet and salute with her trunk. In fact, her old hostility disappeared to such an extent that the park contemplated using her for children's rides.

It is not uncommon for managers to be put in charge of a staff that includes some people whose performance fails to meet their standards but who, for one reason or another, are difficult to move out. Like Tina, they stand in the way of whatever remodeling you have in mind. Yet, also like Tina, some plan for them has to be put into effect before your own plan can get underway. In other words, you've got to do *something*. In a situation like this, here's what you might try:

- *A new opportunity.* It often happens that people with talent and ability are not presented with anything like the challenge they need to produce the best that is in them. They may have been slotted into a limited job by an unsympathetic or vindictive boss, or maneuvered out of the mainstream by a rival, or stigmatized by an unfairly acquired reputation. As someone who is new to the scene, you are in a position to view such people in a fresh light, to take stock of their capabilities, their past accomplishments, their present ideas and interests.

One such manager reports: "I inherited some problem employees when I took over my present responsibilities. One of them—a traffic coordinator—had the reputation of being uncooperative and somewhat abrasive. However, in a conversation, I found her pleasant and interesting to talk to, although a bit defensive. I also found out that she was enrolled in a computer course—I suspect this was because she felt her days with the company were numbered, and she wanted to be prepared to look for work elsewhere. Since I was already planning to computerize much more heavily that we had been, I asked her to do some research. The upshot is that she's now the operation's data processing supervisor and doing quite a job. I haven't heard any more talk about the so-called negative aspects of her personality."

- *A new outlook.* Blockage of opportunity, sameness of work, smallness of expectations—these all tend to produce the kind of boredom that verges on hopelessness, a lack of belief that anything significantly positive can happen on the job. Yet, no matter how deeply affected the employee is by those feelings, studies show that encouragement from above can produce a new direction.

One such encouragement is asking the employee's opinion of what the operation might need to be more effective. Comments a line supervisor who is now deeply involved in his company's quality assurance program: "Instead of simply giving me a production schedule and control sheet, the new general manager asked me how I thought the line could be improved. Then, after I had mentioned a couple of things, he suggested I put them into practice. It's helped a lot to get that kind of support.''

- *A new responsibility.* Yours may be an operation in which employees have been too closely supervised and given too little opportunity for independent action. This sort of constraint can inhibit energy, ideas and the willingness to make a commitment. Often, even a small move away from over-supervision can produce some surprising results. An accountant who now supervises corporate accounts payable says, ''It wasn't until I was put in charge of one customer's accounts payable that I realized how much I enjoyed being my own boss.''

Observation: Some managers assume that their operations are too limited to offer more scope to their employees, and that transfer or termination is the only solution to unsatisfactory performance. Yet, even where the budget is scant, there is something new that can be tried—and be worth the effort.

Adversity Needn't Be Concealed

W ho is the most admired business leader in America? Well, according to the heads of small- and medium-sized businesses who were polled by the Gallup Organization, the answer to that question is Lee Iacocca, the chairman of Chrysler Corporation.

The reason for the choice seems to be a matter of identification. The people questioned are also struggling with the problems of debt and staying alive. And, as Lee Iacocca says, "Misery loves company. If you had taken this poll when I was at Ford, making a billion and half, and I was a fat cat, do you think they'd admire and respect me? Admiration goes up directly proportional to the adversity and ability to deal with it."

Perhaps there is a lesson to be learned from this. Lee Iacocca was not at all reticent about discussing the deep hole Chrysler was in, beset as it was by serious financial and production problems. Nor did he hesitate to talk about the steps he was taking to turn things around. The result was that many people empathized with him.

Too tight a lid. Some managers who are struggling with problems keep everything to themselves. No matter how harassed they may feel, they go around with poker faces. Question them about how things are going and, almost invariably, the answer is, "Everything is fine." Eventually, they may solve their problems, but they don't often get all the credit they deserve. Because of their silence, nobody realizes the depth and complexity of what they have to deal with.

A more rewarding course might be to follow Lee Iacocca's lead and talk about it. There are these benefits to be gained in doing so:

- *Assistance*—suggestions, ideas and advice on how to deal with one or more aspects of the problem.

- *Support*—from those who really understand what is going on.

- *Applause*—when the solution finally goes into effect.

If you decide to follow this course, however, there are certain caveats to keep in mind:

- *Be selective about the problems you do talk about.* Chrysler's Iacocca, for example, didn't talk about the fact that he didn't like one of his new associates or about the trouble they were having with the third bearing from the end on the left rear wheel. Rather, he talked about such problems as the money that must be raised and the concessions that the unions must make. And people listened— and advised.

Use the same tactics yourself—and be selective. Generally, it's the serious problems that require the most assistance. But don't overlook small matters completely. Sometimes, a five-minute talk may clear up a hitch that has bothered you for months.

- *Match your problem with those who can solve it.* Go first to the people who you think can provide some ready advice or assistance. If you're having a budgetary problem, for example, your boss might be the first person you would consult. A problem with another department might call for consultation with someone on your own level. An equipment problem might be more easily dealt with after a talk with one of the people who report to you.

This doesn't preclude talking to any number of other people later. But what you're after is a start in the right direction—and some people are more likely to provide that than others.

- *Go to those in trouble.* Don't hesitate, either, to approach people who may well be having problems of their own. As Lee Iacocca says, "Misery loves company." A discussion about *your* problem may provide a welcome relief for someone with his or her own—and it may lead to the beginning of a solution for both parties.

- *Send out progress bulletins.* You may not be able to appear on television, as Lee Iacocca did to tout Chrysler's progress, but you can keep the people you have talked to up to date on how you are doing. This doesn't have to be done on an everyday basis—perhaps just from one step to another. But doing it provides two benefits. First, you may gain additional assistance in one area or another. Second, and more important, you will be showing people that you *are* in charge, working hard to reach the final solution.

- *Share the applause.* No matter how many people you talked to, no matter how much assistance they provided, it will be your time and effort that are required to put all the pieces together. This could mean that you might be tempted to take a "star turn." Don't. Instead, give credit where it's due—and personally thank everyone who helped you, even in the smallest way. Next time around, you'll be listened to even more closely.

Observation: Action, not a stiff upper lip, is what makes it these days. Confidence is built on a fair amount of openness, not concealment.

How to Handle the Hostility of Others

A lexander Haig left his cabinet post with the reputation of having rubbed a lot of people in government the wrong way. This may not have affected his decision to resign, but there are those who saw it as making his departure much less regrettable than it might have been. Among this group, presumably, were those who might have persuaded him to change his mind and stay.

Usually, whether you're Secretary of State or have a smaller responsibility, it's important to be liked rather than disliked by those on whom you depend to carry out your decisions. It makes your job much easier and allows you to spend your energy on productive matters rather than on trying to figure out why other people—your boss, other managers, your employees—are so mystifyingly uncooperative.

In a study of 21 "derailed" executives made by Morgan W. McCall and Michael M. Lombardo, behavioral scientists at the Center for Creative Leadership, Greensboro, NC, one personality flaw led all the rest. "Insensitivity to others" was the chief reason for these managers failing to go further in their careers.

Avoiding the sore spots. If you sometimes wonder why you are surrounded by oversensitive people who seem bent on taking your every utterance the wrong way, here's what you might consider:

- *Other people's egos are large*—as large as, or possibly larger than, your own. If you ignore them when they need to be recognized, criticize them when they are hoping for praise or demean them when they want support, they are going to perceive your behavior as a threat to their self-esteem. And just as the forces of the body rush to combat an infection, so do the forces of the mind move to defend against a threat to the ego. If you don't foresee such defense building by others or fail to regard it as natural and legitimate, then you might be in for some unpleasant surprises.

- *Other people's sensitivities are extensive,* and it's not a bad idea to do as much mental cataloging of them as possible. If you don't personally know what they might be, ask for some briefing from those who do. This could enable you to take an approach that is less time consuming on the one hand and more productive on the other.

- *Relationships are not static.* Sometimes, they're only as good as your last conversation. It can be dangerous to assume that your relationship with another person is so fine that you no longer have to think about it. It is usually at this point that you find yourself stepping on toes, disregarding sensitivities and incurring resentment.

- *Your words can be upsetting,* unless you take pains to avoid angering those who are affected by them. For instance, if you are about to issue a critique of employee performance, it's better to indicate why it is coming: "I'd like to talk to you about something that I think needs some improvement." You may encounter disagreement, but you lessen the chances that the other person will feel victimized.

- *Negative feelings can escalate*—especially when you wait too long to take ameliorative action after you have made another person angry by making some thoughtless remark. The action doesn't necessarily have to be an apology, but it should at least open the door to a better understanding: "You're angry at me, aren't you?" That way, your initial mistake won't turn into a feud, helped along, perhaps, by your feelings of, "I can be just as angry as he can!"

Observation: Sensitivities are often trampled on by a manager when he or she insists on a course of action without consulting those who will be most affected. Allowing others to change your mind about what you're going to do is not a sign of weakness. Nor is consulting others. Rather, you enable them to feel that they, too, have a voice. This kind of sharing is good management, because it tends to dissolve resentment.

Gripe Sessions Can Be Profitable

" Let's all get together on Tuesday morning for a no-holds-barred discussion. Problems, ideas, gripes—you name it and we'll talk about it.''

This is the kind of directive that many managers send out from time to time, with the hope of some profitable results. But frequently those results don't materialize. The people in the group look at the session as a waste of time. ''It's just something the boss feels has to be done,'' they reason, ''and nothing will come of it anyway.'' So, they keep their important ideas, their real gripes, to themselves. What's the point of making waves?

You may wonder, then, how you can turn people on at a session of this kind and get them to feel that you really want to hear what's on their minds. Here are some suggestions:

- *Keep the meeting small.* The larger the meeting, the easier it is for people who are reluctant to speak up to fade into the crowd. They remain silent while others talk. Yet, they may be just the ones whose ideas and problems should be aired.

It's not easy to ''hide,'' though, at a small meeting; so if you have a large group of people reporting to you, have two or three small sessions rather than one all-inclusive one. You'll get a lot more straight talk, even if you have to prod.

- *Hold the session "in the round."* If there is a round table available at which the group can be seated comfortably, this is ideal. If not, arrange the chairs in a circular fashion. The aim is to have high eye contact, because this leads to maximum interaction. People are much more likely to respond when they can see one another. Furthermore, there is no "head" in a circle. Thus, you fit into the group as a participant rather than as a boss.

- *Listen intently.* This is one situation that you don't want to dominate—it's their talk session, not yours. Still, you don't want to come across as uninvolved or uninterested. So, when someone asks you a question or looks at you expectantly for a response, paraphrase what's been said as you begin your reply. You will be demonstrating your attentiveness—and encouraging further discussion.

- *Put it in writing.* From the very first, take notes—this will indicate to members of the group that you are indeed serious about hearing what they have to say. It can also be viewed as a hopeful sign that you are going to do something about particular items that they mention. You can further strengthen this impression by asking for more details. If there is a complaint, for instance, ask for pertinent details. Then say you'll look into the matter and report back.

- *Use a flipchart or blackboard.* This is a technique that can loosen the tongues of the most reluctant participants. If the discussion is slow in getting started, or if it begins to get bogged down, get up and go to the chart or board. Then lay the groundwork: "Okay, let's get some important points down—just throw out anything that's bothering you, anything at all.''

As you write down the comments, keep your back to the group—you are there simply as an automatic writing instrument. Even if you have to stop and ask, ''Anything else?'' keep your eyes on the chart or board. People often feel less threatened, more at ease and freer to speak their minds when their boss is not facing them directly.

- *Maintain your credibility.* All these factors are important in keeping an ''open'' session alive and kicking. But what about the next one—will it move, too? The answer to that depends on what you do about what you've heard at this session. So, as it draws to a close, review your notes aloud to make sure that you have everything straight. Then follow up on it and report back to the people concerned. This is the insurance for your credibility—and for another meeting that will be just as profitable as the first.

Focus on the Person Who's Got the Job

" Well, I guess this is it," Ed Hansen said to the assembled group, "our fond farewell to Charlie Blake. We're sure going to miss you, Charlie, and we wish you all the best in Arizona."

There was a round of applause and cries of "Hear! Hear!" Then Ed continued, "It's also time, of course, to wish all the best to Charlie's successor, Dave Allen. Welcome aboard, Dave, we're all expecting great things from you. Just keep in mind, though, that you're replacing a legend. Charlie was always the irreplaceable man around here whenever an emergency came up in one of the regions."

Next round. What a way to be welcomed aboard—told by your boss that you're expected to do a great job while following in the footsteps of a legend. Ed Hansen has set his new employee on a rocky path—a mistake that many executives make. They overlook the fact that it is impossible to *replace* any individual. All that can be done is to put another person in the job.

It's true that the newcomer will have a different personality, a different perspective, a different approach. But that certainly doesn't mean a poorer performance than the predecessor. In fact, the newcomer may, in time, do even better, provided that he or she is given the opportunity to develop individual assets and capabilities.

To provide just such an opportunity for an employee who is following an "irreplaceable" predecessor, consider these suggestions:

- *Clarify your position.* There is no reason why you should hide your esteem for a former manager who did a top-notch job, as long as you keep such remarks low-keyed and infrequent. What the newcomer needs, though, is assurance that he or she is not going to be constantly compared to a paragon. So make it clear that the newcomer has your backing—and will be judged on individual merit and progress in the future.

- *Spread the word.* There are a lot of people out there who may have held the newcomer's predecessor in high esteem. Furthermore, they became accustomed to that person's way of doing things. Changes may lead to grumbling—"That's not the way Charlie did it!"—and reluctance to cooperate. It's up to you to make it clear that it's a new ballgame and there's a new manager in the dugout. In short, it's a new start for everybody.

- *Separate the present from the past.* It could be that you and the former employee were personal friends—and if so, there's no need to end that friendship. But don't flaunt it in the vicinity of the successor. For example, a remark that begins with, "I was talking to Charlie yesterday," could, understandably, make the newcomer uneasy. Have you been questioning Charlie, discussing the old and the new? And what conclusions did the two of you reach? Enjoy Charlie's friendship—but keep it private and non-controversial.

- *Provide for alternatives.* Most jobs change over a period of time—a bit is added here, a bit subtracted there. But the general content of the job remains pretty much the same. When you put a newcomer into this position, though, why not try to tailor the job to this person's special talents, perspective and goals? Let's say, for example, that the new employee has special writing skills—you might then delegate some report writing to him or her.

Keep in mind, too, the changing needs of the organization. Both you and the previous holder of the job were used to having certain tasks performed and procedures followed in certain ways. It may be time for some changes to occur in order to meet overall goals more effectively.

Observation: During the first months of the newcomer's tenure, you may find yourself disagreeing with some of the new directions that are being taken. But unless you see any sign of disaster ahead, give Charlie's successor time to move and grow, and succeed in his or her own particular way. If you do, then you may eventually find yourself with another irreplaceable person on your hands.

Newcomers Need Extra Help When They're Starting Out

Y ou have squeezed more money out of a cost-conscious management, and plowed through many, many resumes and interviews to find just the right person to hire for a vital position. But this is only the beginning. The new person you've hired, all too aware of how difficult it has been to find a job, is tense, nervous and cautious. You're loaded with backed-up work and want results immediately. Your staff, overburdened and perhaps anxious about their own jobs, may either expect too much of the new person or attempt to make success difficult.

So, to help the newcomer produce the results you want as smoothly and quickly as possible, you will have to help point the way. Here are some key actions to take:

- *Do the piping aboard personally.* This will indicate your support for the newcomer to your staff. Whether by memo or staff meeting, make three points. The first should be a brief explanation of the background and qualifications the newcomer brings to the job. The second should be an explanation of exactly why he or she was brought in. (This will help allay any fears of rumors of replacement.) The third point should be your expectation of help to be given to the newcomer and how highly your employees' assistance will be valued by you.

- *Conduct an introductory tour.* This is a job too important to delegate. By doing it yourself, you show everyone the importance you place on immediate rapport and a good working relationship. To help establish that relationship as fast as possible, go beyond names and titles as you make introductions and talk about responsibilities each party will have in common and tasks on which they will be working together. That way, they will immediately have something to say to each other beyond "Nice meeting you."

- *Supply more than the standard office essentials.* Make sure the newcomer has such items as an internal phone list, an organizational chart and samples of the organization's products, or reports of its services, as well as any introductory literature or files that are relevant to the job and to the mission of the organization. Also, supply—and explain—work schedules, report forms, work analyses and other essentials.

- *Include the new person in meetings, both formal and informal.* The newcomer can thereby get to see people in action, and thus get to know them. There's also the opportunity—which you should encourage—for the new person to participate. This gives everyone a common base of experience.

- *Look into training possibilities.* If your organization has a training program, find out what might be of use to your new employee. Otherwise, structure your own program for the particular demands of the job. You might, for example, give initial work assignments with an eye to providing the broadest base of experience. Or you might recommend specific reading—books or periodicals that are most immediately relevant. You might also consider providing a guide—a staff member who can take on a mentor-like relationship with the new person.

* *Make sure you maintain regular contact.* The newcomer will need to feel that your door is always open. You might have a regularly scheduled time together—a few minutes of the day or a half-hour or so each week. You can also supplement this with a standing invitation to visit.

Observation: If, like so many managers, you've been working short staffed, then you know how important it is to make sure your new person succeeds. The trouble you take now will have its payoff later.

Good Chemistry Can Improve Credentials

V ince Lombardi once told his team, the Green Bay Packers, "In terms of skill and ability, every one of you is easily replaceable; there are plenty of players around with athletic talent to equal yours." He went on to explain that the quality that distinguished Green Bay from other teams was what he called "character."

Presumably, what Lombardi was talking about was his players' ability to identify with the goals he laid out for the team. The powerful chemistry that developed between the team members and the coach transcended, in Lombardi's view, individual talent and prior professional experience. He saw it as enabling him to get significant extra effort from his players.

What about your team? How can you be certain that future members are going to identify with your goals, as Lombardi's team did with his?

Well, let's start at the beginning. Suppose you're looking for a new assistant—someone who will be a key person. You're going to promote from within and need to decide between two good employees. One has experience and credentials that outshine the other's, but you have a feeling about the second person that you can't ignore. It's not that the first is a bad or especially abrasive individual—it's just that you don't get that traveling-on-the-same-wavelength feeling that you do with the second.

Still, it's easy to be fooled by your feelings, and good credentials are not lightly dismissed. Thus, you don't feel entirely comfortable about a decision that's so subjective. To check whether you're on the right track, ask yourself:

- *What are your reasonable expectations?* The skills that the second person lacks can probably be taught through on-the-job training or outside courses. The payoff will be an assistant with *all* the qualifications, including those you can't define. Can you expect the same of the first person? If the missing ingredient just isn't there, chances are no amount of training will bring it about. You cannot realistically expect a person's basic chemistry to change.

- *What will happen in the long run?* This key person has to be someone you can trust and rely on, because your choice is bound to reflect on the overall quality of your operation. If you see eye to eye on priorities, share a similar approach to problems, have good rapport and just generally click with each other, your confidence will grow. You'll come to feel comfortable delegating responsibilities, knowing they'll be handled in the way you would have handled them yourself. Both of you will benefit. If the chemistry between you is right, you will have more time to be more productive and creative. And your assistant will have more opportunities to be challenged and to grow within the job.

- *What about intangibles?* There are bound to be times when you'll require more than the ordinary from your assistant. This is where sensitivity to your needs and dedication to your goals can make the essential difference between failure and success.

- *What will happen in adversity?* One former Green Bay Packer is quoted as saying: "We got to be Lombardi people; we would only respond to his kind of coaching." When a basic commitment exists, you have more assurance that your assistant's loyalties will lie with you, should office politics or conflicts arise. A good relationship can even take precedence over offers of a more lucrative position within or outside of the organization.

Keys to Successful Living

E very so often, the news media cover a story about a man or woman who has lived to a ripe old age. And, inevitably, each of these senior citizens is asked the same question: "To what do you attribute your longevity?" Just as inevitably, the answers to that question differ. One will say, "No smoking, no drinking, and being in bed every night at nine." Another will say, "A good family, lots of caring and a glass of wine with my dinner." Each, apparently, has found a personal formula for a long and successful life.

At a seminar on mental health, Dr. Barrie Greiff, a psychiatrist who taught at Harvard Business School, offered his formula for living successfully. While it may not add years to your life, it may help you to gain the most from the years ahead.

To live successfully, Dr. Greiff stated, you need:

- *The capacity to love.* Not just romance is needed for longevity. You also need genuine caring and concern for other people. It's important to reach out a helping hand, to give of yourself, to do just a little more. Love, as the song says, makes the world go round—and it also binds people together.

- *The capacity to learn*—from books, from experience, from the world around you. Learning, of necessity, has to be a lifelong process, because changes come so rapidly. An open mind, ready and eager to absorb each new bit of knowledge, is an asset worth cultivating.

- *The capacity to labor.* There are times when a life of idle ease can seem very appealing—nothing to do but relax and enjoy the world around you. Actually, though, it's work—on the job, at home, in a volunteering situation—that provides the real rewards. The sense of satisfaction when you finish a big project, for example, or the feeling of pride when you solve a particularly sticky problem.

- *The capacity to laugh*—at yourself as well as with others. Life can sometimes be hard and dreary. The capacity to see the humor in certain situations, to enjoy the funny side of life, can brighten not only your day but also that of people around you.

- *The capacity to leave.* We all have people and things that we care about very strongly. But the day may come when they are no longer part of our life. A loved one departs, a good job is lost, a valued situation changes for one reason or another. When that time comes, a period of grieving may be in order; but it should soon be set aside. The past is over and done with—it's time to move ahead.

Observation: On first reading, these may seem like rather simple qualities—they do, after all, exist to some degree in all of us. But it's in applying them, in deepening and expanding them, in sustaining them, that truly successful living can occur, now and in the future.